W0115942

CHURCH NOTES

A GUIDED BOOK TO LOG YOUR INNER THOUGHTS

chartwell books

Commit to the Lord whatever you do, and he will establish your plans.

Proverbs 16:3

HOW TO USE THIS BOOK

Sermons are the gentle hand of a shepherd guiding their flock. To really digest their message and receive the most out of their spiritual guidance, this lightly-structured journal for sermon notes will help you foster a deeper relationship to the Bible's teachings and help you remember the favorite parts of your most cherished sermons.

Scheduling a time to reflect and record your thoughts on each sermon is recommended. Once you make a habit out of the activity, deeper meanings will make themselves known. Honing this practice takes time, so if the first sermon notes you fill in do not fill out the space supplied, remind yourself that this is all part of the process. You do not need to have a lot to say about your favorite sermons to receive their blessings.

Record your thoughts after you've listened to your sermon. You are more than welcome to take notes while present if you have trouble remembering the core teachings once you get home. But by letting the sermons sit in your subconscious before pausing to reflect, you have the potential to bring about thoughts that wouldn't have had time to percolate had you simply reflected during service.

Listen to your heart and divine guidance while compiling your thoughts. Some of your journal entries may run off with you, but that is a happy part of internalizing the teachings of each line of scripture and sermon.

Praise the Lord. Give thanks to the Lord, for He is good; His love endures forever.

Psalm 106:1

PASTOR/SPEAKER: DATE:

✧ TODAY'S SERMON ✧

THEME:

SCRIPTURE:

KEY POINTS:

ACCOMPANYING SONGS/HYMNS:

NOTES:

MY REFLECTIONS:

HOW CAN I APPLY TODAY'S SERMON TO MY LIFE?

TODAY I AM GRATEFUL FOR:

But when you ask, you must believe and not doubt, because the one who doubts is like a wave of the sea, blown and tossed by the wind.

JAMES 1:6

PASTOR/SPEAKER: .... DATE: ....

✧ TODAY'S SERMON ✧

THEME:

SCRIPTURE:

KEY POINTS:

ACCOMPANYING SONGS/HYMNS:

NOTES:

MY REFLECTIONS:

HOW CAN I APPLY TODAY'S SERMON TO MY LIFE?

TODAY I AM GRATEFUL FOR:

For God, who said, "Light shall shine out of darkness," is the One who has shone in our hearts to give the Light of the knowledge of the glory of God in the face of Christ.

2 CORINTHIANS 4:6

PASTOR/SPEAKER: DATE:

✧ TODAY'S SERMON ✧

THEME:

SCRIPTURE:

KEY POINTS:

ACCOMPANYING SONGS/HYMNS:

NOTES:

MY REFLECTIONS:

HOW CAN I APPLY TODAY'S SERMON TO MY LIFE?

TODAY I AM GRATEFUL FOR:

God is our refuge and strength, a very present help in trouble. Therefore we will not fear, though the earth should change and though the mountains slip into the heart of the sea; though its waters roar and foam, though the mountains quake at its swelling pride.

PSALM 46:1-3

PASTOR/SPEAKER: .... DATE: ....

✧ TODAY'S SERMON ✧

THEME:

SCRIPTURE:

KEY POINTS:

ACCOMPANYING SONGS/HYMNS:

NOTES:

MY REFLECTIONS:

HOW CAN I APPLY TODAY'S SERMON TO MY LIFE?

TODAY I AM GRATEFUL FOR:

Seek the Lord and His strength; seek His face continually.
Remember His wonderful deeds which He has done, His marvels
and the judgments from His mouth.

1 CHRONICLES 16:11-12

PASTOR/SPEAKER: DATE:

✧ TODAY'S SERMON ✧

THEME:

SCRIPTURE:

KEY POINTS:

ACCOMPANYING SONGS/HYMNS:

NOTES:

MY REFLECTIONS:

HOW CAN I APPLY TODAY'S SERMON TO MY LIFE?

TODAY I AM GRATEFUL FOR:

The Lord is my strength and my shield; my heart trusts in Him, and I am helped; therefore my heart exults, and with my song I shall thank Him.

PSALM 28:7

PASTOR/SPEAKER: .... DATE: ....

✧ Today's Sermon ✧

THEME:

SCRIPTURE:

KEY POINTS:

ACCOMPANYING SONGS/HYMNS:

NOTES:

MY REFLECTIONS:

HOW CAN I APPLY TODAY'S SERMON TO MY LIFE?

TODAY I AM GRATEFUL FOR:

Be strong and courageous, do not be afraid or tremble at them,
for the Lord your God is the one who goes with you.
He will not fail you or forsake you.

DEUTERONOMY 31:6

Be devoted to one another in brotherly love; give preference to one another in honor.

ROMANS 12:10

PASTOR/SPEAKER: DATE:

✧ TODAY'S SERMON ✧

THEME:

SCRIPTURE:

KEY POINTS:

ACCOMPANYING SONGS/HYMNS:

NOTES:

MY REFLECTIONS:

HOW CAN I APPLY TODAY'S SERMON TO MY LIFE?

TODAY I AM GRATEFUL FOR:

Whatever you do in word or deed, do all in the name of the Lord Jesus, giving thanks through Him to God the Father.

COLOSSIANS 3:17

PASTOR/SPEAKER: DATE:

✧ TODAY'S SERMON ✧

THEME:

SCRIPTURE:

KEY POINTS:

ACCOMPANYING SONGS/HYMNS:

NOTES:

MY REFLECTIONS:

HOW CAN I APPLY TODAY'S SERMON TO MY LIFE?

TODAY I AM GRATEFUL FOR:

Now for this very reason also, applying all diligence, in your faith supply moral excellence, and in your moral excellence, knowledge, and in your knowledge, self-control, and in your self-control, perseverance, and in your perseverance, godliness, and in your godliness, brotherly kindness, and in your brotherly kindness, love. For if these qualities are yours and are increasing, they render you neither useless nor unfruitful in the true knowledge of our Lord Jesus Christ.

2 Peter 1:5–8

PASTOR/SPEAKER: .... DATE: ....

✧ TODAY'S SERMON ✧

THEME:

SCRIPTURE:

KEY POINTS:

ACCOMPANYING SONGS/HYMNS:

NOTES:

MY REFLECTIONS:

HOW CAN I APPLY TODAY'S SERMON TO MY LIFE?

TODAY I AM GRATEFUL FOR:

Pursue peace with all men, and the sanctification without which no one will see the Lord.

HEBREWS 12:14

PASTOR/SPEAKER: DATE:

✧ TODAY'S SERMON ✧

THEME:

SCRIPTURE:

KEY POINTS:

ACCOMPANYING SONGS/HYMNS:

NOTES:

MY REFLECTIONS:

HOW CAN I APPLY TODAY'S SERMON TO MY LIFE?

TODAY I AM GRATEFUL FOR:

For by grace you have been saved through faith; and that not of yourselves, it is the gift of God.

EPHESIANS 2:8

PASTOR/SPEAKER: ______________________ DATE: __________

✧ TODAY'S SERMON ✧

THEME:

SCRIPTURE:

KEY POINTS:

ACCOMPANYING SONGS/HYMNS:

NOTES:

MY REFLECTIONS:

HOW CAN I APPLY TODAY'S SERMON TO MY LIFE?

TODAY I AM GRATEFUL FOR:

So I say to you, ask, and it will be given to you; seek, and you will find; knock, and it will be opened to you.

LUKE 11:9

PASTOR/SPEAKER: .... DATE: ....

✧ TODAY'S SERMON ✧

THEME:

SCRIPTURE:

KEY POINTS:

ACCOMPANYING SONGS/HYMNS:

NOTES:

MY REFLECTIONS:

HOW CAN I APPLY TODAY'S SERMON TO MY LIFE?

TODAY I AM GRATEFUL FOR:

And you will know the truth,
and the truth will make you free.

JOHN 8:32

PASTOR/SPEAKER: .... DATE: ....

✧ TODAY'S SERMON ✧

THEME:

SCRIPTURE:

KEY POINTS:

ACCOMPANYING SONGS/HYMNS:

NOTES:

MY REFLECTIONS:

HOW CAN I APPLY TODAY'S SERMON TO MY LIFE?

TODAY I AM GRATEFUL FOR:

In everything I showed you that by working hard in this manner you must help the weak and remember the words of the Lord Jesus, that He Himself said, "It is more blessed to give than to receive."

ACTS 20:35

PASTOR/SPEAKER: .... DATE: ....

✧ TODAY'S SERMON ✧

THEME:

SCRIPTURE:

KEY POINTS:

ACCOMPANYING SONGS/HYMNS:

NOTES:

MY REFLECTIONS:

HOW CAN I APPLY TODAY'S SERMON TO MY LIFE?

TODAY I AM GRATEFUL FOR:

Finally, brethren, whatever is true, whatever is honorable, whatever is right, whatever is pure, whatever is lovely, whatever is of good repute, if there is any excellence and if anything worthy of praise, dwell on these things.

PHILIPPIANS 4:8

PASTOR/SPEAKER: .... DATE: ....

✧ TODAY'S SERMON ✧

THEME:

SCRIPTURE:

KEY POINTS:

ACCOMPANYING SONGS/HYMNS:

NOTES:

MY REFLECTIONS:

HOW CAN I APPLY TODAY'S SERMON TO MY LIFE?

TODAY I AM GRATEFUL FOR:

Cast your burden upon the Lord and He will sustain you;
He will never allow the righteous to be shaken.

PSALM 55:22

Peace I leave with you; My peace I give to you; not as the world gives do I give to you. Do not let your heart be troubled, nor let it be fearful.

John 14:27

PASTOR/SPEAKER: DATE:

✧ TODAY'S SERMON ✧

THEME:

SCRIPTURE:

KEY POINTS:

ACCOMPANYING SONGS/HYMNS:

NOTES:

MY REFLECTIONS:

HOW CAN I APPLY TODAY'S SERMON TO MY LIFE?

TODAY I AM GRATEFUL FOR:

And if you give yourself to the hungry and satisfy the desire of the afflicted, then your light will rise in darkness and your gloom will become like midday.

ISAIAH 58:10

PASTOR/SPEAKER: DATE:

✧ TODAY'S SERMON ✧

THEME:

SCRIPTURE:

KEY POINTS:

ACCOMPANYING SONGS/HYMNS:

NOTES:

MY REFLECTIONS:

HOW CAN I APPLY TODAY'S SERMON TO MY LIFE?

TODAY I AM GRATEFUL FOR:

Be anxious for nothing, but in everything by prayer and supplication with thanksgiving let your requests be made known to God. And the peace of God, which surpasses all comprehension, will guard your hearts and your minds in Christ Jesus.

PHILIPPIANS 4:6-7

PASTOR/SPEAKER: .... DATE: ....

✧ TODAY'S SERMON ✧

THEME:

SCRIPTURE:

KEY POINTS:

ACCOMPANYING SONGS/HYMNS:

NOTES:

MY REFLECTIONS:

HOW CAN I APPLY TODAY'S SERMON TO MY LIFE?

TODAY I AM GRATEFUL FOR:

What use is it, my brethren, if someone says he has faith but he has no works? Can that faith save him? If a brother or sister is without clothing and in need of daily food, and one of you says to them, "Go in peace, be warmed and be filled," and yet you do not give them what is necessary for their body, what use is that? Even so faith, if it has no works, is dead, being by itself.

JAMES 2:14-17

PASTOR/SPEAKER: DATE:

✧ TODAY'S SERMON ✧

THEME:

SCRIPTURE:

KEY POINTS:

ACCOMPANYING SONGS/HYMNS:

NOTES:

MY REFLECTIONS:

HOW CAN I APPLY TODAY'S SERMON TO MY LIFE?

TODAY I AM GRATEFUL FOR:

Now I exhort you, brethren, by the name of our Lord Jesus Christ, that you all agree and that there be no divisions among you, but that you be made complete in the same mind and in the same judgment.

1 Corinthians 1:10

PASTOR/SPEAKER: .... DATE: ....

✧ TODAY'S SERMON ✧

THEME:

SCRIPTURE:

KEY POINTS:

ACCOMPANYING SONGS/HYMNS:

NOTES:

MY REFLECTIONS:

HOW CAN I APPLY TODAY'S SERMON TO MY LIFE?

TODAY I AM GRATEFUL FOR:

There is no fear in love; but perfect love casts out fear, because fear involves punishment, and the one who fears is not perfected in love.

1 JOHN 4:18

PASTOR/SPEAKER: DATE:

✧ TODAY'S SERMON ✧

THEME:

SCRIPTURE:

KEY POINTS:

ACCOMPANYING SONGS/HYMNS:

NOTES:

MY REFLECTIONS:

HOW CAN I APPLY TODAY'S SERMON TO MY LIFE?

TODAY I AM GRATEFUL FOR:

Do not fear, for I am with you; do not anxiously look about you, for I am your God. I will strengthen you, surely I will help you, surely I will uphold you with my righteous right hand.

ISAIAH 41:10

PASTOR/SPEAKER: DATE:

✧ TODAY'S SERMON ✧

THEME:

SCRIPTURE:

KEY POINTS:

ACCOMPANYING SONGS/HYMNS:

NOTES:

MY REFLECTIONS:

HOW CAN I APPLY TODAY'S SERMON TO MY LIFE?

TODAY I AM GRATEFUL FOR:

He who oppresses the poor taunts his Maker,
but he who is gracious to the needy honors Him.

PROVERBS 14:31

PASTOR/SPEAKER: DATE:

✧ TODAY'S SERMON ✧

THEME:

SCRIPTURE:

KEY POINTS:

ACCOMPANYING SONGS/HYMNS:

NOTES:

MY REFLECTIONS:

HOW CAN I APPLY TODAY'S SERMON TO MY LIFE?

TODAY I AM GRATEFUL FOR:

Have I not commanded you? Be strong and courageous! Do not tremble or be dismayed, for the Lord your God is with you wherever you go.

JOSHUA 1:9

PASTOR/SPEAKER: DATE:

✧ TODAY'S SERMON ✧

THEME:

SCRIPTURE:

KEY POINTS:

ACCOMPANYING SONGS/HYMNS:

NOTES:

MY REFLECTIONS:

HOW CAN I APPLY TODAY'S SERMON TO MY LIFE?

TODAY I AM GRATEFUL FOR:

And do not be conformed to this world, but be transformed by the renewing of your mind, so that you may prove what the will of God is, that which is good and acceptable and perfect.

ROMANS 12:2

Whatever you do, do your work heartily, as for the Lord rather than for men, knowing that from the Lord you will receive the reward of the inheritance. It is the Lord Christ whom you serve.

Colossians 3:23–24

PASTOR/SPEAKER: .... DATE: ....

✧ TODAY'S SERMON ✧

THEME:

SCRIPTURE:

KEY POINTS:

ACCOMPANYING SONGS/HYMNS:

NOTES:

MY REFLECTIONS:

HOW CAN I APPLY TODAY'S SERMON TO MY LIFE?

TODAY I AM GRATEFUL FOR:

When pride comes, then comes dishonor.
But with the humble is wisdom.

PROVERBS 11:2

PASTOR/SPEAKER: ______ DATE: ______

✧ TODAY'S SERMON ✧

THEME:

SCRIPTURE:

KEY POINTS:

ACCOMPANYING SONGS/HYMNS:

NOTES:

MY REFLECTIONS:

HOW CAN I APPLY TODAY'S SERMON TO MY LIFE?

TODAY I AM GRATEFUL FOR:

Therefore, having been justified by faith, we have peace with God through our Lord Jesus Christ, through whom also we have obtained our introduction by faith into this grace in which we stand; and we exult in hope of the glory of God.

ROMANS 5:1-2

PASTOR/SPEAKER: .... DATE: ....

✧ TODAY'S SERMON ✧

THEME:

SCRIPTURE:

KEY POINTS:

ACCOMPANYING SONGS/HYMNS:

NOTES:

MY REFLECTIONS:

HOW CAN I APPLY TODAY'S SERMON TO MY LIFE?

TODAY I AM GRATEFUL FOR:

As each one has received a special gift, employ it in serving one another as good stewards of the manifold grace of God.

1 PETER 4:10

PASTOR/SPEAKER: .... DATE: ....

✧ TODAY'S SERMON ✧

THEME:

SCRIPTURE:

KEY POINTS:

ACCOMPANYING SONGS/HYMNS:

NOTES:

MY REFLECTIONS:

HOW CAN I APPLY TODAY'S SERMON TO MY LIFE?

TODAY I AM GRATEFUL FOR:

For God is not unjust so as to forget your work and the love which you have shown toward His name, in having ministered and in still ministering to the saints.

HEBREWS 6:10

PASTOR/SPEAKER: .... DATE: ....

✧ TODAY'S SERMON ✧

THEME:

SCRIPTURE:

KEY POINTS:

ACCOMPANYING SONGS/HYMNS:

NOTES:

MY REFLECTIONS:

HOW CAN I APPLY TODAY'S SERMON TO MY LIFE?

TODAY I AM GRATEFUL FOR:

The generous man will be prosperous,
and he who waters will himself be watered.

PROVERBS 11:25

PASTOR/SPEAKER: ______________________ DATE: __________

✧ TODAY'S SERMON ✧

THEME:

SCRIPTURE:

KEY POINTS:

ACCOMPANYING SONGS/HYMNS:

NOTES:

MY REFLECTIONS:

HOW CAN I APPLY TODAY'S SERMON TO MY LIFE?

TODAY I AM GRATEFUL FOR:

You are altogether beautiful, my darling,
and there is no blemish in you.

SONG OF SOLOMON 4:7

PASTOR/SPEAKER: ______ DATE: ______

✧ TODAY'S SERMON ✧

THEME:

SCRIPTURE:

KEY POINTS:

ACCOMPANYING SONGS/HYMNS:

NOTES:

MY REFLECTIONS:

HOW CAN I APPLY TODAY'S SERMON TO MY LIFE?

TODAY I AM GRATEFUL FOR:

The righteous cry, and the Lord hears and delivers them out of all their troubles. The Lord is near to the brokenhearted and saves those who are crushed in spirit.

PSALM 34:17-18

PASTOR/SPEAKER: DATE:

✧ TODAY'S SERMON ✧

THEME:

SCRIPTURE:

KEY POINTS:

ACCOMPANYING SONGS/HYMNS:

NOTES:

MY REFLECTIONS:

HOW CAN I APPLY TODAY'S SERMON TO MY LIFE?

TODAY I AM GRATEFUL FOR:

Be kind to one another, tender-hearted, forgiving each other, just as God in Christ also has forgiven you.

EPHESIANS 4:32

PASTOR/SPEAKER: DATE:

✧ TODAY'S SERMON ✧

THEME:

SCRIPTURE:

KEY POINTS:

ACCOMPANYING SONGS/HYMNS:

NOTES:

MY REFLECTIONS:

HOW CAN I APPLY TODAY'S SERMON TO MY LIFE?

TODAY I AM GRATEFUL FOR:

We have come to know and have believed the love which God has for us. God is love, and the one who abides in love abides in God, and God abides in him.

1 JOHN 4:16

Yet those who wait for the Lord will gain new strength; They will mount up with wings like eagles, they will run and not get tired, they will walk and not become weary.

Isaiah 40:31

PASTOR/SPEAKER: .... DATE: ....

✧ TODAY'S SERMON ✧

THEME:

SCRIPTURE:

KEY POINTS:

ACCOMPANYING SONGS/HYMNS:

NOTES:

MY REFLECTIONS:

HOW CAN I APPLY TODAY'S SERMON TO MY LIFE?

TODAY I AM GRATEFUL FOR:

Blessed is a man who perseveres under trial, for once he has been approved, he will receive the crown of life which the Lord has promised to those who love Him.

JAMES 1:12

PASTOR/SPEAKER: DATE:

✧ TODAY'S SERMON ✧

THEME:

SCRIPTURE:

KEY POINTS:

ACCOMPANYING SONGS/HYMNS:

NOTES:

MY REFLECTIONS:

HOW CAN I APPLY TODAY'S SERMON TO MY LIFE?

TODAY I AM GRATEFUL FOR:

So, as those who have been chosen of God, holy and beloved,
put on a heart of compassion, kindness, humility, gentleness, and patience.

COLOSSIANS 3:12

PASTOR/SPEAKER: .... DATE: ....

✧ TODAY'S SERMON ✧

THEME:

SCRIPTURE:

KEY POINTS:

ACCOMPANYING SONGS/HYMNS:

NOTES:

MY REFLECTIONS:

HOW CAN I APPLY TODAY'S SERMON TO MY LIFE?

TODAY I AM GRATEFUL FOR:

When I am afraid, I will put my trust in You. In God, whose word I praise,
in God I have put my trust; I shall not be afraid.
What can mere men do to me?

PSALM 56:3-4

PASTOR/SPEAKER: ______ DATE: ______

✧ Today's Sermon ✧

THEME:

SCRIPTURE:

KEY POINTS:

ACCOMPANYING SONGS/HYMNS:

NOTES:

MY REFLECTIONS:

HOW CAN I APPLY TODAY'S SERMON TO MY LIFE?

TODAY I AM GRATEFUL FOR:

Truly, truly, I say to you, a slave is not greater than his master, nor is one who is sent greater than the one who sent him.

JOHN 13:16

PASTOR/SPEAKER: .... DATE: ....

✧ TODAY'S SERMON ✧

THEME:

SCRIPTURE:

KEY POINTS:

ACCOMPANYING SONGS/HYMNS:

NOTES:

MY REFLECTIONS:

HOW CAN I APPLY TODAY'S SERMON TO MY LIFE?

TODAY I AM GRATEFUL FOR:

Therefore encourage one another and build up one another, just as you also are doing.

1 Thessalonians 5:11

PASTOR/SPEAKER: .... DATE: ....

✧ TODAY'S SERMON ✧

THEME:

SCRIPTURE:

KEY POINTS:

ACCOMPANYING SONGS/HYMNS:

NOTES:

MY REFLECTIONS:

HOW CAN I APPLY TODAY'S SERMON TO MY LIFE?

TODAY I AM GRATEFUL FOR:

For wisdom will enter your heart and knowledge will be pleasant to your soul; discretion will guard you, understanding will watch over you.

PROVERBS 2:10–11

PASTOR/SPEAKER: .... DATE: ....

✧ TODAY'S SERMON ✧

THEME:

SCRIPTURE:

KEY POINTS:

ACCOMPANYING SONGS/HYMNS:

NOTES:

MY REFLECTIONS:

HOW CAN I APPLY TODAY'S SERMON TO MY LIFE?

TODAY I AM GRATEFUL FOR:

Behold, how good and how pleasant it is for brothers to dwell together in unity!

PSALM 133:1

PASTOR/SPEAKER: .... DATE: ....

✧ TODAY'S SERMON ✧

THEME:

SCRIPTURE:

KEY POINTS:

ACCOMPANYING SONGS/HYMNS:

NOTES:

MY REFLECTIONS:

HOW CAN I APPLY TODAY'S SERMON TO MY LIFE?

TODAY I AM GRATEFUL FOR:

"For I know the plans that I have for you," declares the Lord. "Plans for welfare and not for calamity to give you a future and a hope."

JEREMIAH 29:11

PASTOR/SPEAKER: DATE:

✧ TODAY'S SERMON ✧

THEME:

SCRIPTURE:

KEY POINTS:

ACCOMPANYING SONGS/HYMNS:

NOTES:

MY REFLECTIONS:

HOW CAN I APPLY TODAY'S SERMON TO MY LIFE?

TODAY I AM GRATEFUL FOR:

Your ears will hear a word behind you, "This is the way, walk in it," whenever you turn to the right or to the left.

ISAIAH 30:21

The Lord is not slow
about His promise, as
some count slowness,
but is patient toward
you, not wishing for
any to perish but
for all to come
to repentance.

2 Peter 3:9

PASTOR/SPEAKER: .... DATE: ....

✧ TODAY'S SERMON ✧

THEME:

SCRIPTURE:

KEY POINTS:

ACCOMPANYING SONGS/HYMNS:

NOTES:

MY REFLECTIONS:

HOW CAN I APPLY TODAY'S SERMON TO MY LIFE?

TODAY I AM GRATEFUL FOR:

Love is patient, love is kind and is not jealous;
love does not brag and is not arrogant.

1 CORINTHIANS 13:4

PASTOR/SPEAKER: DATE:

✧ TODAY'S SERMON ✧

THEME:

SCRIPTURE:

KEY POINTS:

ACCOMPANYING SONGS/HYMNS:

NOTES:

MY REFLECTIONS:

HOW CAN I APPLY TODAY'S SERMON TO MY LIFE?

TODAY I AM GRATEFUL FOR:

Come to Me, all who are weary and heavy-laden,
and I will give you rest.

MATTHEW 11:28

PASTOR/SPEAKER: DATE:

✧ TODAY'S SERMON ✧

THEME:

SCRIPTURE:

KEY POINTS:

ACCOMPANYING SONGS/HYMNS:

NOTES:

MY REFLECTIONS:

HOW CAN I APPLY TODAY'S SERMON TO MY LIFE?

TODAY I AM GRATEFUL FOR:

For we are His workmanship, created in Christ Jesus for good works, which God prepared beforehand so that we would walk in them.

EPHESIANS 2:10

PASTOR/SPEAKER: DATE:

✧ TODAY'S SERMON ✧

THEME:

SCRIPTURE:

KEY POINTS:

ACCOMPANYING SONGS/HYMNS:

NOTES:

MY REFLECTIONS:

HOW CAN I APPLY TODAY'S SERMON TO MY LIFE?

TODAY I AM GRATEFUL FOR:

Listen to counsel and accept discipline,
that you may be wise the rest of your days.

PROVERBS 19:20

PASTOR/SPEAKER: DATE:

✧ TODAY'S SERMON ✧

THEME:

SCRIPTURE:

KEY POINTS:

ACCOMPANYING SONGS/HYMNS:

NOTES:

MY REFLECTIONS:

HOW CAN I APPLY TODAY'S SERMON TO MY LIFE?

TODAY I AM GRATEFUL FOR:

Two are better than one because they have a good return for their labor. For if either of them falls, the one will lift up his companion. But woe to the one who falls when there is not another to lift him up.

ECCLESIASTES 4:9–10

PASTOR/SPEAKER: .... DATE: ....

✧ TODAY'S SERMON ✧

THEME:

SCRIPTURE:

KEY POINTS:

ACCOMPANYING SONGS/HYMNS:

NOTES:

MY REFLECTIONS:

HOW CAN I APPLY TODAY'S SERMON TO MY LIFE?

TODAY I AM GRATEFUL FOR:

We love,
because He first loved us.

1 John 4:19

PASTOR/SPEAKER: DATE:

✧ TODAY'S SERMON ✧

THEME:

SCRIPTURE:

KEY POINTS:

ACCOMPANYING SONGS/HYMNS:

NOTES:

MY REFLECTIONS:

HOW CAN I APPLY TODAY'S SERMON TO MY LIFE?

TODAY I AM GRATEFUL FOR:

Therefore if anyone is in Christ, he is a new creature;
the old things passed away; behold, new things have come.

2 Corinthians 5:17

PASTOR/SPEAKER: DATE:

✧ TODAY'S SERMON ✧

THEME:

SCRIPTURE:

KEY POINTS:

ACCOMPANYING SONGS/HYMNS:

NOTES:

MY REFLECTIONS:

HOW CAN I APPLY TODAY'S SERMON TO MY LIFE?

TODAY I AM GRATEFUL FOR:

Give, and it will be given to you. They will pour into your lap a good measure—pressed down, shaken together, and running over. For by your standard of measure it will be measured to you in return.

LUKE 6:38

PASTOR/SPEAKER: ………………………… DATE: …………

✧ Today's Sermon ✧

THEME:

SCRIPTURE:

KEY POINTS:

ACCOMPANYING SONGS/HYMNS:

NOTES:

MY REFLECTIONS:

HOW CAN I APPLY TODAY'S SERMON TO MY LIFE?

TODAY I AM GRATEFUL FOR:

And the Word became flesh, and dwelt among us, and we saw His glory, glory as of the only begotten from the Father, full of grace and truth.

JOHN 1:14

It is the Spirit who gives life; the flesh profits nothing; the words that I have spoken to you are spirit and are life.

John 6:63

PASTOR/SPEAKER: DATE:

✧ TODAY'S SERMON ✧

THEME:

SCRIPTURE:

KEY POINTS:

ACCOMPANYING SONGS/HYMNS:

NOTES:

MY REFLECTIONS:

HOW CAN I APPLY TODAY'S SERMON TO MY LIFE?

TODAY I AM GRATEFUL FOR:

But grow in the grace and knowledge of our Lord and Savior Jesus Christ. To Him be the glory, both now and to the day of eternity.

2 Peter 3:18

PASTOR/SPEAKER: .... DATE: ....

✧ Today's Sermon ✧

THEME:

SCRIPTURE:

KEY POINTS:

ACCOMPANYING SONGS/HYMNS:

NOTES:

MY REFLECTIONS:

HOW CAN I APPLY TODAY'S SERMON TO MY LIFE?

TODAY I AM GRATEFUL FOR:

When I was a child, I used to speak like a child, think like a child, reason like a child; when I became a man, I did away with childish things.

1 CORINTHIANS 13:11

PASTOR/SPEAKER: .... DATE: ....

✧ TODAY'S SERMON ✧

THEME:

SCRIPTURE:

KEY POINTS:

ACCOMPANYING SONGS/HYMNS:

NOTES:

MY REFLECTIONS:

HOW CAN I APPLY TODAY'S SERMON TO MY LIFE?

TODAY I AM GRATEFUL FOR:

But the goal of our instruction is love from a pure heart and a good conscience and a sincere faith.

1 Timothy 1:5

PASTOR/SPEAKER: .... DATE: ....

✧ TODAY'S SERMON ✧

THEME:

SCRIPTURE:

KEY POINTS:

ACCOMPANYING SONGS/HYMNS:

NOTES:

MY REFLECTIONS:

HOW CAN I APPLY TODAY'S SERMON TO MY LIFE?

TODAY I AM GRATEFUL FOR:

If we confess our sins, He is faithful and righteous to forgive us our sins and to cleanse us from all unrighteousness.

1 John 1:9

PASTOR/SPEAKER: .... DATE: ....

✧ TODAY'S SERMON ✧

THEME:

SCRIPTURE:

KEY POINTS:

ACCOMPANYING SONGS/HYMNS:

NOTES:

MY REFLECTIONS:

HOW CAN I APPLY TODAY'S SERMON TO MY LIFE?

TODAY I AM GRATEFUL FOR:

Not forsaking our own assembling together, as is the habit of some, but encouraging one another; and all the more as you see the day drawing near.

HEBREWS 10:25

PASTOR/SPEAKER: DATE:

✧ TODAY'S SERMON ✧

THEME:

SCRIPTURE:

KEY POINTS:

ACCOMPANYING SONGS/HYMNS:

NOTES:

MY REFLECTIONS:

HOW CAN I APPLY TODAY'S SERMON TO MY LIFE?

TODAY I AM GRATEFUL FOR:

But we all, with unveiled face, beholding as in a mirror the glory of the Lord, are being transformed into the same image from glory to glory, just as from the Lord, the Spirit.

2 Corinthians 3:18

PASTOR/SPEAKER: DATE:

✧ TODAY'S SERMON ✧

THEME:

SCRIPTURE:

KEY POINTS:

ACCOMPANYING SONGS/HYMNS:

NOTES:

MY REFLECTIONS:

HOW CAN I APPLY TODAY'S SERMON TO MY LIFE?

TODAY I AM GRATEFUL FOR:

For there is one God, and one mediator also between God and men, the man Christ Jesus, who gave Himself as a ransom for all, the testimony given at the proper time.

1 Timothy 2:5-6

PASTOR/SPEAKER: .... DATE: ....

✧ Today's Sermon ✧

THEME:

SCRIPTURE:

KEY POINTS:

ACCOMPANYING SONGS/HYMNS:

NOTES:

MY REFLECTIONS:

HOW CAN I APPLY TODAY'S SERMON TO MY LIFE?

TODAY I AM GRATEFUL FOR:

But store up for yourselves treasures in heaven, where neither moth nor rust destroys, and where thieves do not break in or steal; for where your treasure is, there your heart will be also.

MATTHEW 6:20-21

PASTOR/SPEAKER: .... DATE: ....

✧ TODAY'S SERMON ✧

THEME:

SCRIPTURE:

KEY POINTS:

ACCOMPANYING SONGS/HYMNS:

NOTES:

MY REFLECTIONS:

HOW CAN I APPLY TODAY'S SERMON TO MY LIFE?

TODAY I AM GRATEFUL FOR:

Be of the same mind toward one another; do not be haughty in mind, but associate with the lowly. Do not be wise in your own estimation.

ROMANS 12:16

The mind of the prudent acquires knowledge, and the ear of the wise seeks knowledge.

Proverbs 18:15

PASTOR/SPEAKER: DATE:

✧ Today's Sermon ✧

THEME:

SCRIPTURE:

KEY POINTS:

ACCOMPANYING SONGS/HYMNS:

NOTES:

MY REFLECTIONS:

HOW CAN I APPLY TODAY'S SERMON TO MY LIFE?

TODAY I AM GRATEFUL FOR:

Little children, let us not love with word or with tongue, but in deed and truth.

1 JOHN 3:18

PASTOR/SPEAKER: DATE:

✧ TODAY'S SERMON ✧

THEME:

SCRIPTURE:

KEY POINTS:

ACCOMPANYING SONGS/HYMNS:

NOTES:

MY REFLECTIONS:

HOW CAN I APPLY TODAY'S SERMON TO MY LIFE?

TODAY I AM GRATEFUL FOR:

And hope does not disappoint, because the love of God has been poured out within our hearts through the Holy Spirit who was given to us.

ROMANS 5:5

PASTOR/SPEAKER: DATE:

✧ TODAY'S SERMON ✧

THEME:

SCRIPTURE:

KEY POINTS:

ACCOMPANYING SONGS/HYMNS:

NOTES:

MY REFLECTIONS:

HOW CAN I APPLY TODAY'S SERMON TO MY LIFE?

TODAY I AM GRATEFUL FOR:

Let all that you do be done in love.

1 Corinthians 16:14

PASTOR/SPEAKER: DATE:

✧ TODAY'S SERMON ✧

THEME:

SCRIPTURE:

KEY POINTS:

ACCOMPANYING SONGS/HYMNS:

NOTES:

MY REFLECTIONS:

HOW CAN I APPLY TODAY'S SERMON TO MY LIFE?

TODAY I AM GRATEFUL FOR:

I have been crucified with Christ; and it is no longer I who live, but Christ lives in me; and the life which I now live in the flesh I live by faith in the Son of God, who loved me and gave Himself up for me.

GALATIANS 2:20

PASTOR/SPEAKER: .... DATE: ....

✧ TODAY'S SERMON ✧

THEME:

SCRIPTURE:

KEY POINTS:

ACCOMPANYING SONGS/HYMNS:

NOTES:

MY REFLECTIONS:

HOW CAN I APPLY TODAY'S SERMON TO MY LIFE?

TODAY I AM GRATEFUL FOR:

But the wisdom from above is first pure, then peaceable, gentle, reasonable, full of mercy and good fruits, unwavering, without hypocrisy.

JAMES 3:17

PASTOR/SPEAKER: ______ DATE: ______

✧ TODAY'S SERMON ✧

THEME:

SCRIPTURE:

KEY POINTS:

ACCOMPANYING SONGS/HYMNS:

NOTES:

MY REFLECTIONS:

HOW CAN I APPLY TODAY'S SERMON TO MY LIFE?

TODAY I AM GRATEFUL FOR:

Therefore I say to you, all things for which you pray and ask, believe that you have received them, and they will be granted you.

MARK 11:24

PASTOR/SPEAKER: DATE:

✧ TODAY'S SERMON ✧

THEME:

SCRIPTURE:

KEY POINTS:

ACCOMPANYING SONGS/HYMNS:

NOTES:

MY REFLECTIONS:

HOW CAN I APPLY TODAY'S SERMON TO MY LIFE?

TODAY I AM GRATEFUL FOR:

But if we walk in the light as He Himself is in the light, we have fellowship with one another, and the blood of Jesus His Son cleanses us from all sin.

1 JOHN 1:7

PASTOR/SPEAKER: DATE:

✧ Today's Sermon ✧

THEME:

SCRIPTURE:

KEY POINTS:

ACCOMPANYING SONGS/HYMNS:

NOTES:

MY REFLECTIONS:

HOW CAN I APPLY TODAY'S SERMON TO MY LIFE?

TODAY I AM GRATEFUL FOR:

By wisdom a house is built, and by understanding it is established; and by knowledge the rooms are filled with all precious and pleasant riches.

PROVERBS 24:3-4

PASTOR/SPEAKER: .... DATE: ....

✧ TODAY'S SERMON ✧

THEME:

SCRIPTURE:

KEY POINTS:

ACCOMPANYING SONGS/HYMNS:

NOTES:

MY REFLECTIONS:

HOW CAN I APPLY TODAY'S SERMON TO MY LIFE?

TODAY I AM GRATEFUL FOR:

Therefore, prepare your minds for action, keep sober in spirit, fix your hope completely on the grace to be brought to you at the revelation of Jesus Christ.

1 PETER 1:13

Open your mouth,
judge righteously,
and defend the
rights of
the afflicted
and needy.

Proverbs 31:9

PASTOR/SPEAKER: .... DATE: ....

✧ TODAY'S SERMON ✧

THEME:

SCRIPTURE:

KEY POINTS:

ACCOMPANYING SONGS/HYMNS:

NOTES:

MY REFLECTIONS:

HOW CAN I APPLY TODAY'S SERMON TO MY LIFE?

TODAY I AM GRATEFUL FOR:

Your word is a lamp to my feet and a light to my path. I have sworn and I will confirm it, that I will keep Your righteous ordinances.

PSALM 119:105–106

PASTOR/SPEAKER: DATE:

✧ TODAY'S SERMON ✧

THEME:

SCRIPTURE:

KEY POINTS:

ACCOMPANYING SONGS/HYMNS:

NOTES:

MY REFLECTIONS:

HOW CAN I APPLY TODAY'S SERMON TO MY LIFE?

TODAY I AM GRATEFUL FOR:

And now I commend you to God and to the word of His grace, which is able to build you up and to give you the inheritance among all those who are sanctified.

ACTS 20:32

PASTOR/SPEAKER: DATE:

✧ TODAY'S SERMON ✧

THEME:

SCRIPTURE:

KEY POINTS:

ACCOMPANYING SONGS/HYMNS:

NOTES:

MY REFLECTIONS:

HOW CAN I APPLY TODAY'S SERMON TO MY LIFE?

TODAY I AM GRATEFUL FOR:

Sanctify them in the truth;
your word is truth.

JOHN 17:17

PASTOR/SPEAKER: .... DATE: ....

✧ TODAY'S SERMON ✧

THEME:

SCRIPTURE:

KEY POINTS:

ACCOMPANYING SONGS/HYMNS:

NOTES:

MY REFLECTIONS:

HOW CAN I APPLY TODAY'S SERMON TO MY LIFE?

TODAY I AM GRATEFUL FOR:

Whom have I in heaven but You? And besides You, I desire nothing on earth. My flesh and my heart may fail, but God is the strength of my heart and my portion forever.

PSALM 73:25-26

PASTOR/SPEAKER: DATE:

✧ TODAY'S SERMON ✧

THEME:

SCRIPTURE:

KEY POINTS:

ACCOMPANYING SONGS/HYMNS:

NOTES:

MY REFLECTIONS:

HOW CAN I APPLY TODAY'S SERMON TO MY LIFE?

TODAY I AM GRATEFUL FOR:

Then the dust will return to the earth as it was,
and the spirit will return to God who gave it.

ECCLESIASTES 12:7

PASTOR/SPEAKER: .... DATE: ....

✧ TODAY'S SERMON ✧

THEME:

SCRIPTURE:

KEY POINTS:

ACCOMPANYING SONGS/HYMNS:

NOTES:

MY REFLECTIONS:

HOW CAN I APPLY TODAY'S SERMON TO MY LIFE?

TODAY I AM GRATEFUL FOR:

The Lord is the one who goes ahead of you; He will be with you. He will not fail you or forsake you. Do not fear or be dismayed.

DEUTERONOMY 31:8

PASTOR/SPEAKER: .... DATE: ....

✧ TODAY'S SERMON ✧

THEME:

SCRIPTURE:

KEY POINTS:

ACCOMPANYING SONGS/HYMNS:

NOTES:

MY REFLECTIONS:

HOW CAN I APPLY TODAY'S SERMON TO MY LIFE?

TODAY I AM GRATEFUL FOR:

To sum up, all of you be harmonious, sympathetic, brotherly, kindhearted, and humble in spirit.

1 PETER 3:8

PASTOR/SPEAKER: .... DATE: ....

✧ TODAY'S SERMON ✧

THEME:

SCRIPTURE:

KEY POINTS:

ACCOMPANYING SONGS/HYMNS:

NOTES:

MY REFLECTIONS:

HOW CAN I APPLY TODAY'S SERMON TO MY LIFE?

TODAY I AM GRATEFUL FOR:

Is anyone among you suffering? Then he must pray.
Is anyone cheerful? He is to sing praises.

JAMES 5:13

PASTOR/SPEAKER: .... DATE: ....

✧ TODAY'S SERMON ✧

THEME:

SCRIPTURE:

KEY POINTS:

ACCOMPANYING SONGS/HYMNS:

NOTES:

MY REFLECTIONS:

HOW CAN I APPLY TODAY'S SERMON TO MY LIFE?

TODAY I AM GRATEFUL FOR:

Oil and perfume make the heart glad, So a man's counsel is sweet to his friend.

PROVERBS 27:9

The good man out of the good treasure of his heart brings forth what is good; and the evil man out of the evil treasure brings forth what is evil; for his mouth speaks from that which fills his heart.

Luke 6:45

PASTOR/SPEAKER: .... DATE: ....

✧ TODAY'S SERMON ✧

THEME:

SCRIPTURE:

KEY POINTS:

ACCOMPANYING SONGS/HYMNS:

NOTES:

MY REFLECTIONS:

HOW CAN I APPLY TODAY'S SERMON TO MY LIFE?

TODAY I AM GRATEFUL FOR:

In Him we have redemption through His blood, the forgiveness of our trespasses, according to the riches of His grace.

EPHESIANS 1:7

PASTOR/SPEAKER: .... DATE: ....

✧ Today's Sermon ✧

THEME:

SCRIPTURE:

KEY POINTS:

ACCOMPANYING SONGS/HYMNS:

NOTES:

MY REFLECTIONS:

HOW CAN I APPLY TODAY'S SERMON TO MY LIFE?

TODAY I AM GRATEFUL FOR:

For He rescued us from the domain of darkness, and transferred us to the kingdom of His beloved Son.

COLOSSIANS 1:13

PASTOR/SPEAKER: DATE:

✧ TODAY'S SERMON ✧

THEME:

SCRIPTURE:

KEY POINTS:

ACCOMPANYING SONGS/HYMNS:

NOTES:

MY REFLECTIONS:

HOW CAN I APPLY TODAY'S SERMON TO MY LIFE?

TODAY I AM GRATEFUL FOR:

As far as the east is from the west, so far has
He removed our transgressions from us.

PSALM 103:12

PASTOR/SPEAKER: DATE:

✧ TODAY'S SERMON ✧

THEME:

SCRIPTURE:

KEY POINTS:

ACCOMPANYING SONGS/HYMNS:

NOTES:

MY REFLECTIONS:

HOW CAN I APPLY TODAY'S SERMON TO MY LIFE?

TODAY I AM GRATEFUL FOR:

Be diligent to present yourself approved to God as a workman who does not need to be ashamed, accurately handling the word of truth.

2 Timothy 2:15

PASTOR/SPEAKER: DATE:

✧ Today's Sermon ✧

THEME:

SCRIPTURE:

KEY POINTS:

ACCOMPANYING SONGS/HYMNS:

NOTES:

MY REFLECTIONS:

HOW CAN I APPLY TODAY'S SERMON TO MY LIFE?

TODAY I AM GRATEFUL FOR:

You will seek Me and find Me when you search for Me with all your heart.

JEREMIAH 29:13

PASTOR/SPEAKER: DATE:

✧ TODAY'S SERMON ✧

THEME:

SCRIPTURE:

KEY POINTS:

ACCOMPANYING SONGS/HYMNS:

NOTES:

MY REFLECTIONS:

HOW CAN I APPLY TODAY'S SERMON TO MY LIFE?

TODAY I AM GRATEFUL FOR:

Do this, knowing the time, that it is already the hour for you to awaken from sleep; for now salvation is nearer to us than when we believed.

ROMANS 13:11

PASTOR/SPEAKER: DATE:

✧ TODAY'S SERMON ✧

THEME:

SCRIPTURE:

KEY POINTS:

ACCOMPANYING SONGS/HYMNS:

NOTES:

MY REFLECTIONS:

HOW CAN I APPLY TODAY'S SERMON TO MY LIFE?

TODAY I AM GRATEFUL FOR:

He who conceals his transgressions will not prosper,
but he who confesses and forsakes them will find compassion.

PROVERBS 28:13

PASTOR/SPEAKER: .... DATE: ....

✧ TODAY'S SERMON ✧

THEME:

SCRIPTURE:

KEY POINTS:

ACCOMPANYING SONGS/HYMNS:

NOTES:

MY REFLECTIONS:

HOW CAN I APPLY TODAY'S SERMON TO MY LIFE?

TODAY I AM GRATEFUL FOR:

No temptation has overtaken you but such as is common to man; and God is faithful, who will not allow you to be tempted beyond what you are able, but with the temptation will provide the way of escape also, so that you will be able to endure it.

1 CORINTHIANS 10:13

PASTOR/SPEAKER: .... DATE: ....

✧ Today's Sermon ✧

THEME:

SCRIPTURE:

KEY POINTS:

ACCOMPANYING SONGS/HYMNS:

NOTES:

MY REFLECTIONS:

HOW CAN I APPLY TODAY'S SERMON TO MY LIFE?

TODAY I AM GRATEFUL FOR:

Blessed be the God and Father of our Lord Jesus Christ, who according to His great mercy has caused us to be born again to a living hope through the resurrection of Jesus Christ from the dead.

1 Peter 1:3

PASTOR/SPEAKER: .... DATE: ....

✧ Today's Sermon ✧

THEME:

SCRIPTURE:

KEY POINTS:

ACCOMPANYING SONGS/HYMNS:

NOTES:

MY REFLECTIONS:

HOW CAN I APPLY TODAY'S SERMON TO MY LIFE?

TODAY I AM GRATEFUL FOR:

Arise, shine; for your light has come,
and the glory of the Lord has risen upon you.

ISAIAH 60:1

PASTOR/SPEAKER: ______________________ DATE: __________

✧ TODAY'S SERMON ✧

THEME:

SCRIPTURE:

KEY POINTS:

ACCOMPANYING SONGS/HYMNS:

NOTES:

MY REFLECTIONS:

HOW CAN I APPLY TODAY'S SERMON TO MY LIFE?

TODAY I AM GRATEFUL FOR:

My son, do not forget my teaching,
but let your heart keep my commandments; for length of days
and years of life and peace they will add to you.

PROVERBS 3:1-2

PASTOR/SPEAKER: .... DATE: ....

✧ TODAY'S SERMON ✧

THEME:

SCRIPTURE:

KEY POINTS:

ACCOMPANYING SONGS/HYMNS:

NOTES:

MY REFLECTIONS:

HOW CAN I APPLY TODAY'S SERMON TO MY LIFE?

TODAY I AM GRATEFUL FOR:

Let no unwholesome word proceed from your mouth, but only such a word as is good for edification according to the need of the moment, so that it will give grace to those who hear.

EPHESIANS 4:29

First published in 2021 as *Sermon Notes* by Chartwell Books,,
an imprint of The Quarto Group
142 West 36th Street, 4th Floor
New York, NY 10018 USA
T (212) 779-4972
www.Quarto.com

This edition published in 2025 by Chartwell Books, an imprint of The Quarto Group.

Chartwell titles are also available at discount for retail, wholesale, promotional, and bulk purchase. For details, contact the Special Sales Manager by email at specialsales@quarto.com or by mail at The Quarto Group, Attn: Special Sales Manager, 100 Cummings Center Suite 265D, Beverly, MA 01915, USA.

10 9 8 7 6 5 4 3 2 1

ISBN: 978-0-7858-4732-8

Publisher: Rage Kindelsperger
Creative Director: Laura Drew
Managing Editor: Cara Donaldson
Project Editor: Leeann Moreau
Cover and Interior Design: B. Middleworth

Printed in China